Tonal Sight-Singing, The Book

Asaf Peres

Copyright © 2013 by Asaf Peres

All rights reserved. This book or any portion thereof
may not be reproduced or used in any manner whatsoever
without the express written permission of the publisher
except for the use of brief quotations in a book review.

For comments, inquiries, and suggestions please email **info@tonalsightsinging.com**

Printed in the United States of America

First Printing, 2013

ISBN-13: 978-1482744965

ISBN-10: 1482744961

About *Tonal Sight-Singing, the Book*

This is the first of a series of three books that are intended to help aspiring musicians in their quest for achieving proficiency in tonal sight-singing. This first book will cover mostly diatonic music, though towards the end it touches on stepwise chromatic motion and some basic modulations. It is designed for the first year of the two-year aural skills sequence of college music majors, but it is also suitable for non music majors taking an aural skills class, as well as high school music students.

Books II and III will be more advanced and are designed for the second year of the aural-skills sequence and advanced courses. Book II will deal with chromatic scale-degrees (i.e. $\sharp\hat{4}$, $\flat\hat{6}$, etc.) in a manner similar to the way Book I deals with the diatonic collection. Book III will start exploring the subtleties of how the scale-degrees work in different contexts of local harmony, and will include exercises for dealing with alterations in the music caused by other parts.

There are many aspects to aural skills, but I have decided to focus these books on the skill of tonal sight-singing, and specifically the aspect of pitch, which is what most students in aural skills classes struggle with. I have experienced these struggles myself as an undergraduate student. When I started teaching this subject, I felt the need to come up with a method of teaching that would address these difficulties, so that I would have a better chance of helping my students

The Method

One of my main goals, when working on this method, was to free my students from the common tendency to rely on the intervals between adjacent notes as their main tool for sight-singing. Although one can enjoy some success by relying on adjacent intervals, especially when dealing with sequences and other familiar intervallic patterns, it becomes increasingly difficult to rely on this method when the music becomes more complex and incorporates less predictable melodic patterns.

Another problem that arises when attempting to rely on local melodic intervals is that, for example, a perfect fourth between $\hat{5}$ and $\hat{1}$ may sound completely different from a perfect fourth between $\hat{3}$ and $\hat{6}$. Even the same two notes, say G and B, sound very different in the key of C major than they do in B minor.

About *Tonal Sight-Singing, the Book*

Like many teachers, I want my students to learn the unique sound and tendencies of each scale-degree, rather than rely on intervals. The problem is that it's hard to get your hands on music that lets you focus on one specific scale-degree. In light of this fact, I decided to use my skills as a composer and write melodies that would enable focusing on specific scale-degrees, and hopefully be enjoyable to sing. Soon enough, I had written such a large number of melodies and exercises, that the decision to write a book was almost inevitable, so here we are now.

The introduction of the scale-degrees in this book is progressive. After introducing the concept of the tonal system and tonal center, I start with the dominant scale-degree ($\hat{5}$), and keep moving through the diatonic collection until all scale-degrees are covered. More details on the structure of the chapters and how the drills work are in the next section: *How to Use this Book*.

On Solfège-Syllable Systems

While I do have my preferences, this book intentionally refrains from choosing one solfège-syllable system over the other. The two most prevalent systems today are the fixed-do and movable-do systems. Each has its strengths and weaknesses, but both are suitable for utilizing with the methods presented in this book. The only place in the book where I address this issue is chapter 3 – when working on the warm-up exercise, I find it best to avoid the solfège-syllable systems altogether and use the names of the notes instead. Otherwise, feel free to use any system you like.

How to Use this Book

Please read this. It's important!

For beginners

Tonal Sight-Singing, the Book assumes basic prior knowledge of clefs (treble and bass), rhythm, time signatures, keys, and some music theory terminology. If you have never heard of these terms before, you should probably familiarize yourself with them before you dive into sight singing. If you are familiar with these terms but lack proficiency in some areas, you can certainly learn from this book and use it as a tool to improve your level of proficiency. I suggest the following steps:

- Clefs – If you are having trouble reading music from a certain clef, I would advise that before you attempt to sing a melody, go through the notes and say their names out loud. Repeat this several times until you are confident that you can identify each note within a reasonable timeframe.
- Rhythm and times signatures – Make sure you understand the difference between simple meter ($\frac{2}{4}$, $\frac{3}{4}$, etc.) and compound meter ($\frac{6}{8}$, $\frac{9}{8}$, etc.). Take time to recite the rhythm of each melody before you try to sing the pitches. Study the rhythmic patterns and pay attention to rhythmic repetitions.
- Keys and key signatures – Before starting to sing a melody, take time to make sure that you are aware of the key it is in, and map out the scale-degrees of that key.
- Chord structure – Each chapter begins with a brief explanation of the characteristics of the discussed scale degree. Knowing how chords are constructed in tonal music will help you understand this introduction, and provide better context for the exercises.

The structure of the book and how to get the most out of it

Most chapters in this book are designed to help you memorize the sound of a specific scale-degree within the tonal system. A typical chapter starts with a brief discussion of the scale-degree, and continues with two very short melodic fragments that are easy to memorize. Combining these two fragments creates a longer melodic fragment with a leap to the scale-degree that is the focus of the chapter. So, for example, in chapter 4, which deals with the dominant scale-degree ($\hat{5}$), the combined melody will include a leap to $\hat{5}$.

How to Use this Book

After that, a series of one-measure "mini-melodies" follows. If we take chapter 4 as our example again, these short melodies will all feature leaps **to** $\hat{5}$ from different scale-degrees, allowing you to practice and further establish the sound of $\hat{5}$ in your mind. It is advisable to repeat each of these melodies at least twice or until you feel comfortable that you can sing it fluently.

Once you are done with those, the real fun starts. You will encounter a series of longer melodies that include leaps to the featured scale-degree, as well as leaps to scale-degrees that were studied in previous chapters. These melodies will also be in various keys and time signatures. It is advisable to take a moment to prepare yourself before starting each new melody. Sing an arpeggio or a scale to orient your ear to the key. Try to spot all the different appearances of the featured scale-degree in the melody. Count a couple of measures to get used to the time signature.

Start singing the melody **as slowly as you need** in order to do it fluently, without stopping, then repeat, slightly picking up the tempo with each repetition. Don't be shy about practicing in tempi that seem excessively slow. In fact, practicing in slow motion (not only in sight singing, but also in instrumental performance) is one of the most important habits you can pick up, as it allows you to be aware and in control of every detail that goes into your performance.

I suggest mixing up your practice methods. Devote a period of time to actually sight-singing different melodies, while working thoroughly on a single melody at another time. It even wouldn't be a bad idea to jump ahead in the book and try out some more advanced melodies. Occasionally testing your ability to handle challenges that require skills you have not yet mastered has its merits.

Of course, the melodies in this book are "laboratory melodies", composed with the method in mind. As you learn and improve, it would be wise to try your hand at music from the "real world". It can be music of any tonal style (although one can adopt certain aspects of this method for studying atonal music, it is tailored towards tonal music), including classical (in the broad sense), jazz, popular, and any other music that relies on a tonal system.

Finally, although my ego would want me to say that this book will teach you everything you need in order to master sight singing, I believe that learning is not necessarily a linear process, and that any perspective you can gain from familiarizing yourself with other methods and approaches is certainly worth exploring.

I hope you find this book helpful and enjoyable. Good luck!

Table of Contents

About Tonal Sight-Singing, the Book……………………………………..i

How to Use this Book………………………………………………………iii

1. Matching Pitch……………………………………………………..1
2. Establishing Tonality and Stepwise Motion…………………….4
3. Introduction to Scale-Degrees………………………………….10
4. The Dominant ($\hat{5}$) in Major Keys……………………………..16
5. The Dominant ($\hat{5}$) in Minor Keys……………………………..21
6. Compound Melody……………………………………………….25
7. The Supertonic ($\hat{2}$) in Major Keys……………………………..28
8. The Supertonic ($\hat{2}$) in Minor Keys……………………………..33
9. The Leading Tone ($\hat{7}$) in Major Keys…………………………38
10. The Leading Tone ($\hat{7}$) in Minor Keys…………………………45
11. The Subtonic ($\flat\hat{7}$) in Minor Keys……………………………..51
12. The Tonic ($\hat{1}$) in Major Keys……………………………………56
13. The Tonic ($\hat{1}$) in Minor Keys……………………………………62
14. The Subdominant ($\hat{4}$) in Major Keys………………………….67
15. The Subdominant ($\hat{4}$) in Minor Keys………………………….73
16. The Submediant ($\hat{6}$) in Major Keys……………………………78
17. The Submediant ($\hat{6}$) in Minor Keys……………………………84
18. The Mediant ($\hat{3}$) in Major Keys…………………………………90
19. The Mediant ($\hat{3}$) in Minor Keys…………………………………96
20. Stepwise Chromatic Motion……………………………………101
21. Tonicization and Modulations to Closely Related Keys………..106

Acknowledgements……………………………………………………..110

1. Matching Pitch

Matching pitch – the ability to reproduce a pitch that you hear internally or externally – is a crucial skill for those who wish to learn how to sight sing. While lacking the ability to accurately repeat a pitch vocally does not necessarily indicate that one is unable to hear the pitch correctly, gaining that skill allows us to provide ourselves with proper feedback, which is essential for making significant progress.

This is a short but extremely important chapter. It will consist of a set of brief guidelines on practicing matching pitch. You may already have enough experience or the natural ability to accurately match pitch. If that is the case, feel free to skip this chapter. Otherwise, give yourself enough time to practice these exercises and master pitch-matching. It will save you a lot of trouble later on.

Preparation

Ideally, you should practice in a quiet room with a piano, or any other pitched instrument that does not require your mouth to play it (for the purposes of this book, we will assume that we are using a piano). It's best to have some kind of recording device, so you can listen to yourself after attempting to perform the exercises and evaluate your progress. It doesn't have to be anything fancy. Your smart-phone will do. If you don't have a recording device, ask a friend to listen to you and check if the pitches you are producing vocally are the same pitches you are trying to match.

Exercises

<u>Single Pitch</u>

The first thing to do is to play a note on the piano. I like to start with middle C, but you can choose any note you feel comfortable singing. Listen to the note for a few seconds, and then try to sing the exact pitch that you are hearing. Listen to the recording (or have a friend indicate your level of success). If you were not able to match the pitch, try slowly moving towards it by changing your own pitch until you can match the piano's.

If after a while this didn't work, you can try a different approach – try singing a random pitch, and then look for it on the piano by playing different keys until you are able to find the one that plays the exact same pitch that you are singing. Keep checking yourself, or have your friend check you.

1. Matching Pitch

Next, try the same procedure on a different pitch. Move around the piano and try to match as many different pitches as possible. Make sure you breathe properly before trying to sing each pitch, especially when you attempt pitches in less comfortable vocal ranges.

There are different ways to get there, but the important thing is to reach the point where you are singing the exact same pitch as the one that is being played on the piano. Once you are able to do that, keep playing and singing that pitch simultaneously, and listen. Make sure that you feel the difference between the sound of the synchronized pitches and the sound you were previously hearing, before you were successful in reproducing the desired pitch.

Consecutive Pitches

If you feel comfortable with matching single pitches, now is the time to move on and try matching a series of pitches, or a melodic line/fragment. Start with very short (2-3 notes) fragments, at an extremely slow tempo. Play and listen to the notes, and then try singing along while playing. Try these two fragments:

1.a

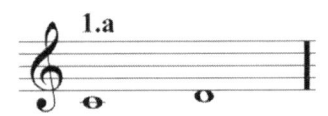

1.b

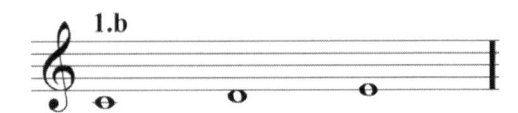

Now, try going up and down using these fragments, like this:

1.c

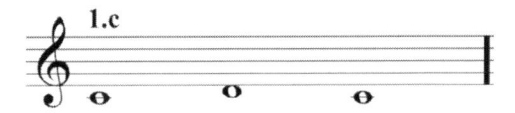

1.d

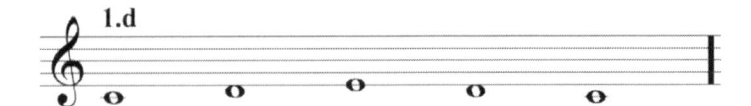

1. Matching Pitch

Of course, you can make up your own fragments and note combinations. So far we have used C as the implied tonal center, but you can use any note you want. Once you feel comfortable singing several consecutive pitches in stepwise motion, you can start skipping around, either diatonically or chromatically. For example:

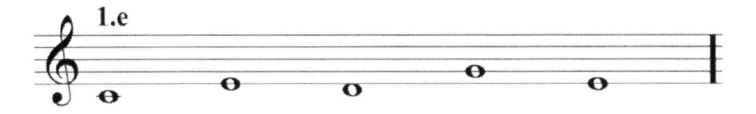

1.e

Or:

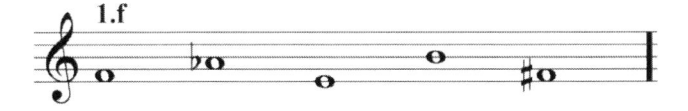

1.f

Feel free to make up any combinations you can think of. Keep challenging yourself until you can match any pitch or combination of pitches within your vocal range. Once you feel comfortable doing that, you are ready to move on.

2. Establishing Tonality and Stepwise Motion

In this chapter we will first practice singing scales, as well as singing in stepwise motion from different points in the scales. Once again, this is a crucial skill, because being able to do this means you have a strong sense of the tonality and of the role each scale-degree plays within it.

Although music from different periods may feature many types of modes, we will focus primarily of the major and minor, which are relevant to the overwhelming majority of Western music literature (including contemporary popular music).

Major

Let's start with major scales. Sing the following scales up and down. You can play along at first, to make sure you are accurately matching every pitch.

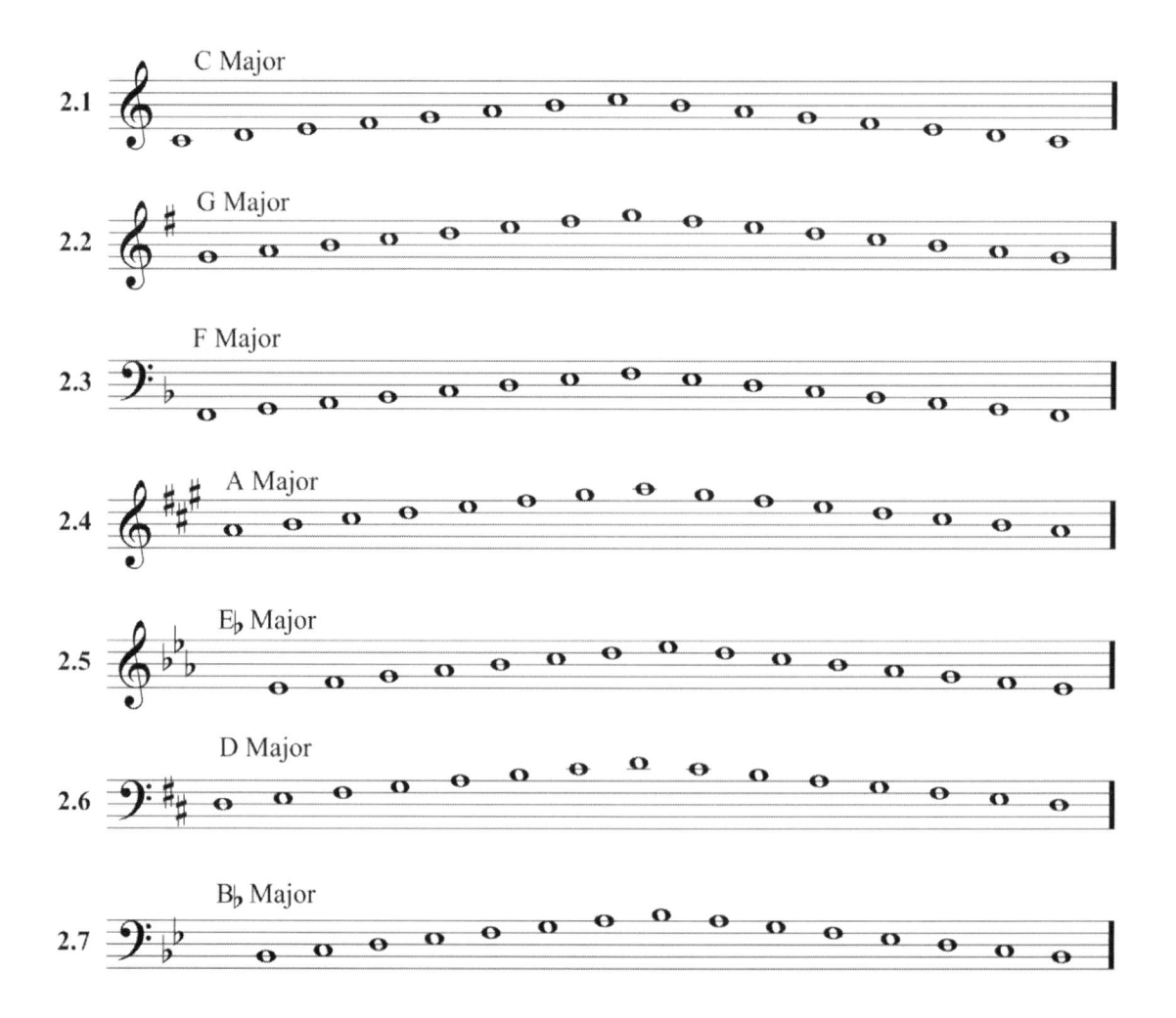

2.1 C Major

2.2 G Major

2.3 F Major

2.4 A Major

2.5 E♭ Major

2.6 D Major

2.7 B♭ Major

2. Establishing Tonality and Stepwise Motion

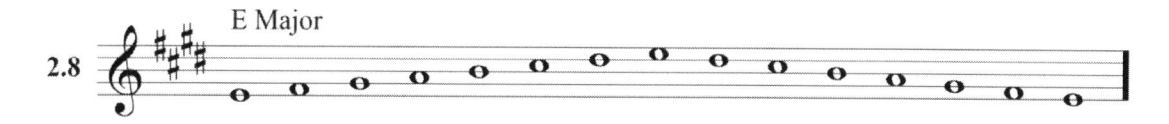

2.8 [E Major musical notation]

Let's now take a look at the following melodic progressions. These progressions move mostly in stepwise motion but will include occasional skips. In these exercises, try to sing the stepwise portion on your own, but when there is a skip, you can play the note you are skipping to, and once again continue the stepwise motion by yourself. The purpose of this is to reinforce the feeling of tonal orientation. If you are able to accurately follow a stepwise progression from any given scale-degree, this means that you have a strong grasp of the tonality, and you are ready to start getting to know each scale-degree on a more intimate level.

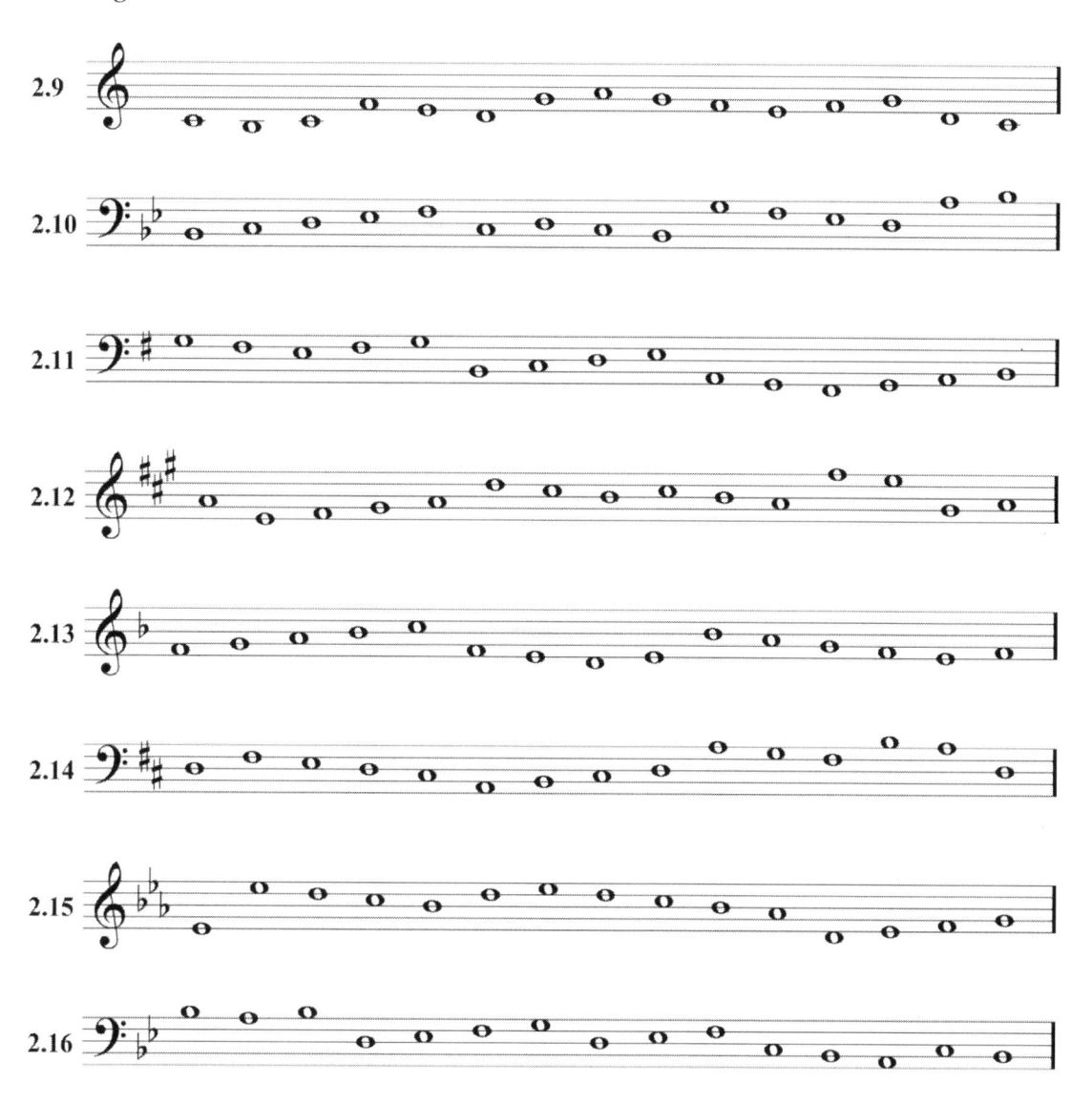

2.9

2.10

2.11

2.12

2.13

2.14

2.15

2.16

2. Establishing Tonality and Stepwise Motion

2.17

Minor

If you are now able to comfortably orient yourself within the major tonality, it is time to move to the minor mode. The same principles apply here, but the minor mode also has two common "mutations": The Harmonic Minor and Melodic Minor.

In the harmonic minor, the seventh scale-degree is raised by a half-step in order to create a leading tone, which is not present in the natural minor and is often necessary for establishing a minor tonality. The melodic minor features both a raised sixth and seventh scale-degrees. This is for the purpose of creating an upwards, stepwise melodic motion, which consists of a leading tone resolving to the tonic, but avoids the augmented second that occurs between the sixth and seventh scale-degrees in the harmonic minor. However, when moving downwards, in most cases the sixth and seventh scale degrees will return to their natural position, since there is no need for a leading tone. This is why when practicing melodic minor scales we typically go back to the natural minor when moving downwards. Here are the three types of minor scales, all with a tonal center of C:

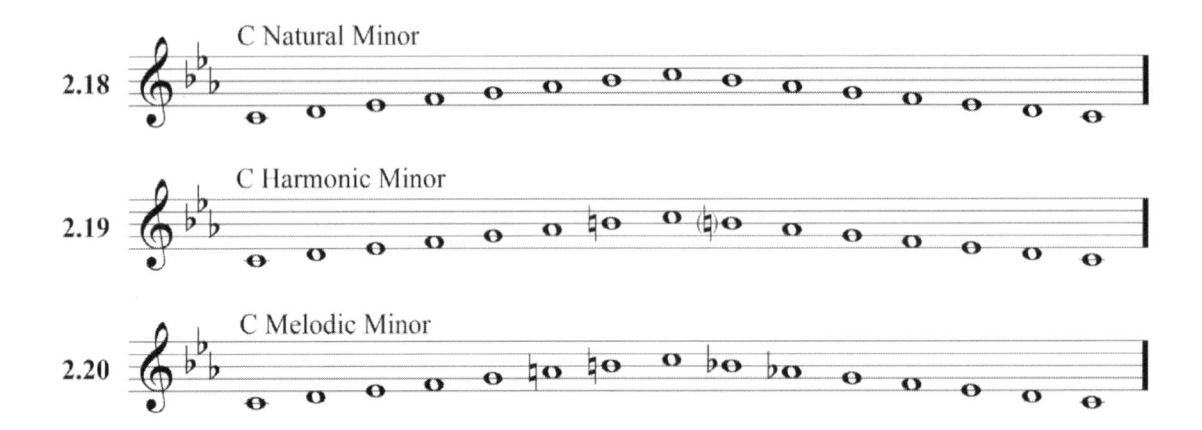

2.18 C Natural Minor

2.19 C Harmonic Minor

2.20 C Melodic Minor

Note that while these are different types of scales, they are not different types of **keys**. You would be hard-pressed to find a piece written "in D harmonic minor". The melodic and harmonic minor are "mutations" that occur naturally within a piece, according to the circumstances, as described above, which is why the raising of the scale degrees is done

2. Establishing Tonality and Stepwise Motion

using accidentals (most typically ♭ or ♮) in the body of the music, and **never** in the key signature.

Let's try to sing a few more minor scales. Notice that these will be of all three types. In addition to learning the sound of the natural minor scale, we have to really become familiar with the different melodic motions created in the harmonic and melodic minor scales. Mostly, we want to become proficient in recognizing and singing the augmented second that occurs between the sixth and (raised) seventh scale-degrees in harmonic minor, as well as the swift switching between the melodic and natural minor motion when going up and down the melodic minor scale:

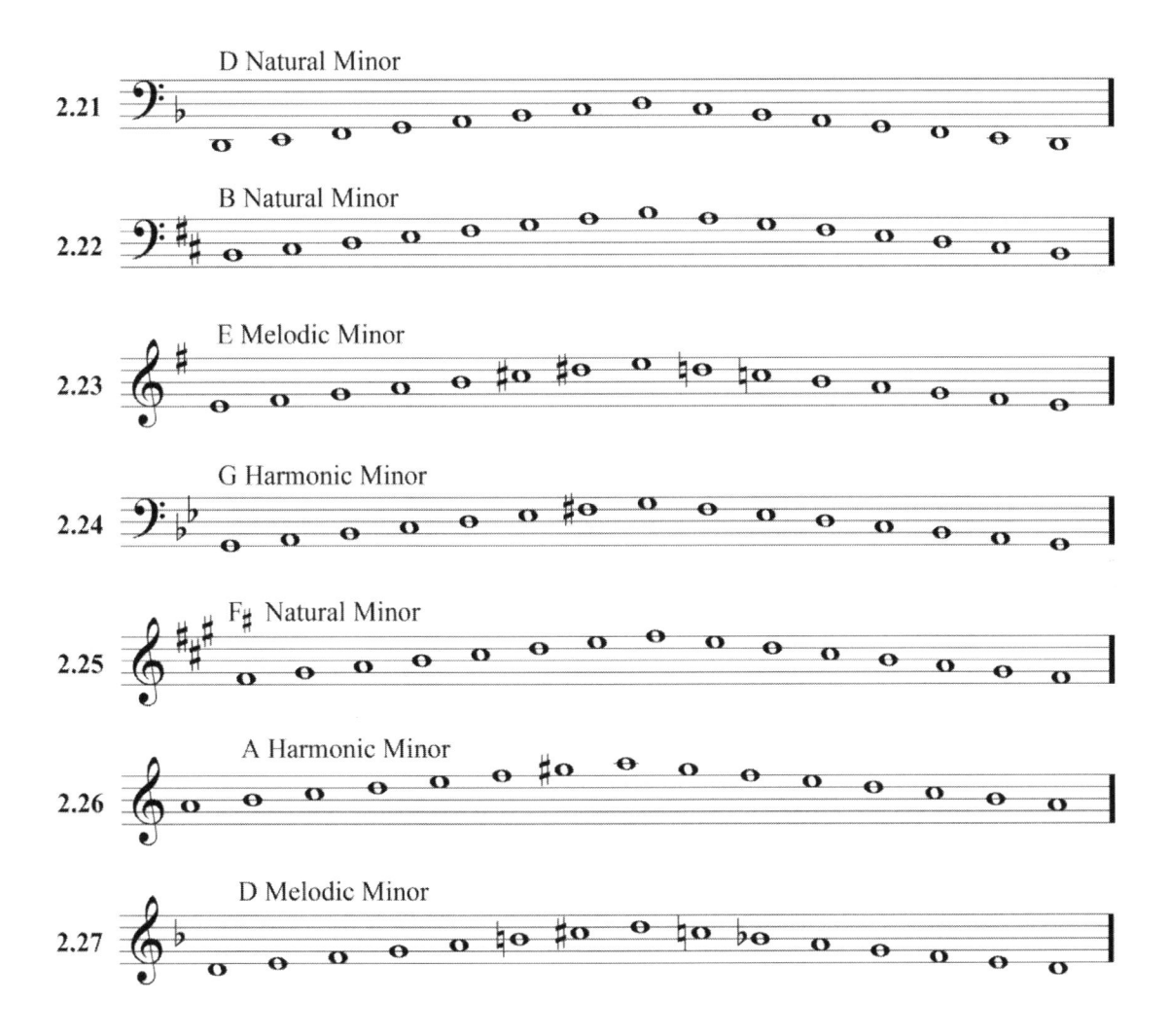

2.21 D Natural Minor

2.22 B Natural Minor

2.23 E Melodic Minor

2.24 G Harmonic Minor

2.25 F♯ Natural Minor

2.26 A Harmonic Minor

2.27 D Melodic Minor

2. Establishing Tonality and Stepwise Motion

Now, just like we did with the major scales, let's try to sing some melodic progressions in minor. When a note is skipped to, you can play that note, match it, and then try to proceed on your own with the stepwise motion. Remember to pay attention to the types of melodic motion near the tonic. **Is it natural, harmonic, or melodic minor type of motion?**

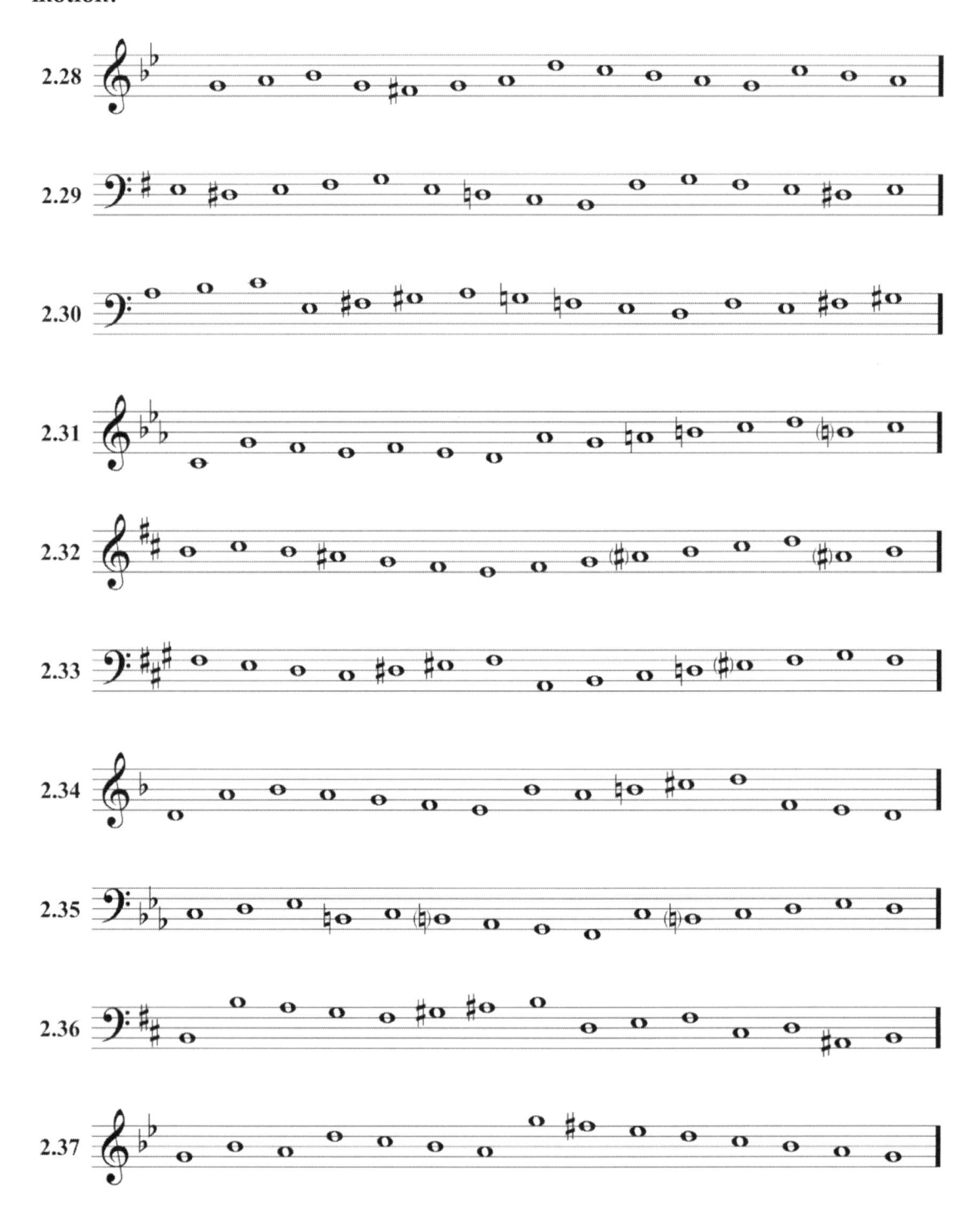

2. Establishing Tonality and Stepwise Motion

Hopefully, you can now confidently sing in stepwise motion from any note in a given tonality. If you are not sure, I suggest you repeat the above exercises until you are. If you are ready, we can now move on and start familiarizing ourselves with the different scale-degrees of the major and minor tonalities.

3. Introduction to the Scale-Degrees

And a Basic Tool to Start Tackling Your Favorite Music

In the previous chapter, we started singing melodies that featured mostly stepwise motion, but also incorporated some skips. We gave ourselves some "training wheels" by playing along with the notes that were skipped to, but now it's time to start working towards freeing ourselves from these training wheels. The way to do this is to gradually become familiar with the sound of each scale-degree in the major and minor tonalities.

In this book, the melodies are tailored to help you study the sound of each scale-degree individually, so that by the end you can master all of them and possess the ability to hear and sight-sing tonal music. However, "real" music does not normally take a step-by-step approach similar to this, so if you want to start singing Mozart, Brahms, The Beatles, Lady Gaga, etc. (which I expect you do, even if not everyone on this list…), you will need some basic tools that will enable you to tackle this music at some level, even if your skills are not completely refined yet.

Let's first take a look at the different scale-degrees in the tonal collection. Each scale-degree has a different role, or tendency, in the tension/release system that makes up the tonal system. These tendencies can be temporarily altered. For example, the tonic, which is the most stable tone, can become unstable when sounding simultaneously with a dominant below it in the bass, and take on a temporary tendency that directs it towards the leading tone, which is temporarily stable in that context (as in a cadential $^6_4$ chord, or a suspended V chord). However, in the vast majority of tonal music, the tendency of each scale-degree will eventually, if not immediately, be resolved, thus it is important to keep in mind the most prevailing characteristics of each scale-degree:

- **Tonic ($\hat{1}$)** – The first scale-degree, and the most important one of all. It is the point of reference, according to which the roles of all the other scale-degrees are defined. The tonic is considered to be the most stable note in the diatonic collection, and any tension that is built up in a piece of tonal music is expected to ultimately find its resolution in it (although in some types of music it does not).
- **Supertonic ($\hat{2}$)** – The upper-neighbor to the tonic, which is the reason for its name. The supertonic may have several different roles in local contexts, but is generally considered a relatively unstable tone and is ultimately expected to resolve to the tonic.

3. Introduction to the Scale-Degrees

- **Mediant ($\hat{3}$)** – The mediant, placed midway between the tonic and dominant scale-degrees, is considered a relatively stable tone. As the middle note of the tonic triad, it usually serves to define whether the tonic (and therefore the local tonality, in most cases) is major or minor.
- **Subdominant ($\hat{4}$)** – The fourth scale-degree is called the subdominant, due to its placement, a perfect fifth below the tonic (as opposed to the dominant, which is placed a perfect fifth above the tonic). The subdominant triad often serves as a "springboard" of sorts to the dominant triad on the way to a cadence (authentic or half-cadence). However, the placement of the subdominant scale-degree a seventh above the dominant scale-degree, a tritone from the leading tone, and a half step above the mediant (in major), causes it to frequently be used as the seventh of the dominant chord, escalating tension and instability, and creating stronger expectations for a resolution to the tonic triad.
- **Dominant ($\hat{5}$)** – The second most important scale-degree (after the tonic) in the diatonic collection. The $\hat{5}$-$\hat{1}$ motion in the bass is often the mark of an authentic cadence (an important tool for marking significant arrival points and establishing the tonality), comprised of the dominant (or dominant seventh) chord, followed by the tonic triad.
- **Submediant ($\hat{6}$)** – Midway between the subdominant and the tonic, the submediant typically pulls towards the dominant. This is especially true in minor, where the submediant is only a half step above the dominant (as opposed to a full step in major), and serves as sort of an upper leading tone to the dominant. Similarly to the mediant, the submediant is also a factor in distinguishing between major and minor tonalities.
- **Leading-Tone ($\hat{7}$)** – Located a half step below the tonic, and therefore "leads" to a resolution. The leading-tone is such an important motion tool in the tonal system, that even in a minor tonality the seventh scale-degree is often altered (raised by a half-step) in order to create a leading-tone. Its role within the dominant triad is crucial for effective cadences.

Scale-Degree Exercise

To start getting familiar with the sound of each scale-degree, we will perform a simple but very effective exercise (and one of my favorites), which I was introduced to during my undergraduate studies and have used ever since as a teacher, much to the joy (?) of my students. I recommend you use this exercise for warming up whenever you practice sight-singing.

3. Introduction to the Scale-Degrees

The sequence is simple, but **please read the instructions carefully in order to make sure that the exercise is effective** (a short summary is provided at the end of the chapter as well):

We will start by choosing a key. As with pretty much any exercise in this book, I will begin with C Major as our starting point, but you will be free to choose any key you want after you get the hang of this exercise and do it on your own. In fact, I recommend that you start every practice session with about 5 minutes of this exercise, and do it in a different key each time.

After choosing a key, we will play the tonic (since we chose C major, we will start with the note C) on the piano, in the middle register, and immediately sing it back, in whatever register is most comfortable for us: If you have a baritone voice you might sing it an octave lower than it sounds on the piano, and if you are a soprano you may prefer to sing it an octave higher.

For the purposes of <u>this exercise</u>, my suggestion is to abandon any solfège-syllable system you are using and just sing back the name of the note.

Next, we will play the same note (C) several times, but each time in a different register (chosen randomly), while singing back after each note **in the same register you began with**. The series of notes you play on the piano will look something like this:

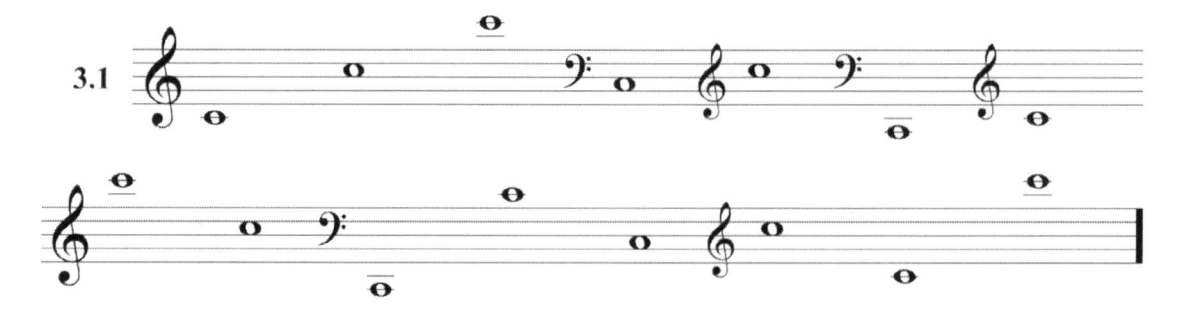

3.1

However, the series of notes you sing back will look like this:

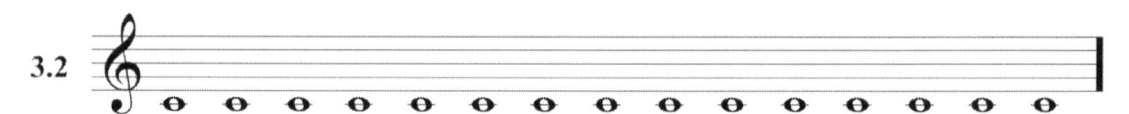

3.2

3. Introduction to the Scale-Degrees

The next step is to gradually add more notes, one by one for each set. First I add scale-degree $\hat{5}$, so the series of notes you sing back, **regardless of which registers you choose to play them in**, will look roughly like this:

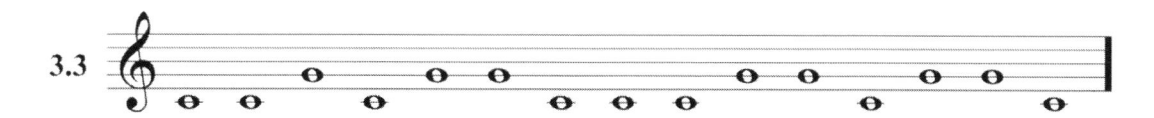

3.3

> **Remember**: While the notes you sing back are in a limited register, as demonstrated above, the notes you play on the piano will be in different, random registers. The idea is for you to hear each note as a functional note within the given tonality, without relying on the intervals between the pairs of adjacent notes.

Next, we add $\hat{2}$:

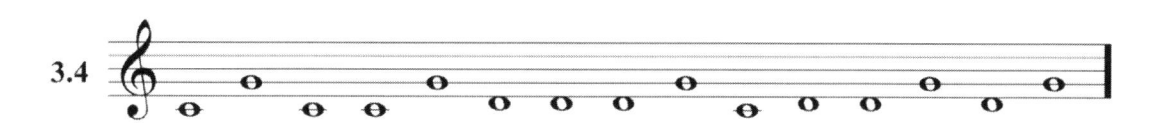

3.4

The next note I usually add is $\hat{7}$ (the Leading Tone). As we add more notes the sets become gradually longer, so that each note receives sufficient representation in the set:

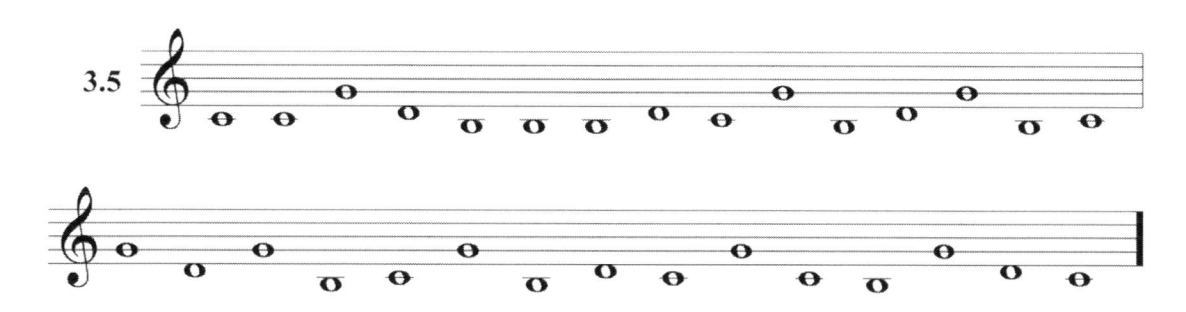

3.5

We keep adding notes gradually (the typical order of appearance in my sets is $\hat{1}$-$\hat{5}$-$\hat{2}$-$\hat{7}$-$\hat{4}$-$\hat{6}$-$\hat{3}$) until we eventually practice sets with the entire diatonic collection, like this one:

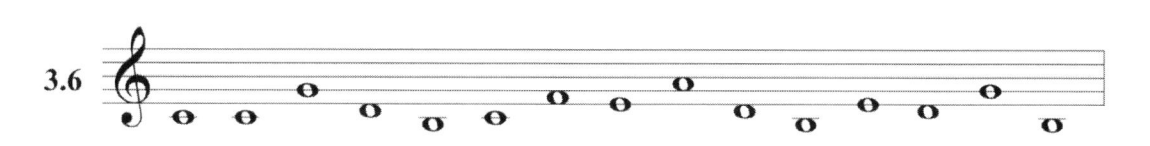

3.6

3. Introduction to the Scale-Degrees

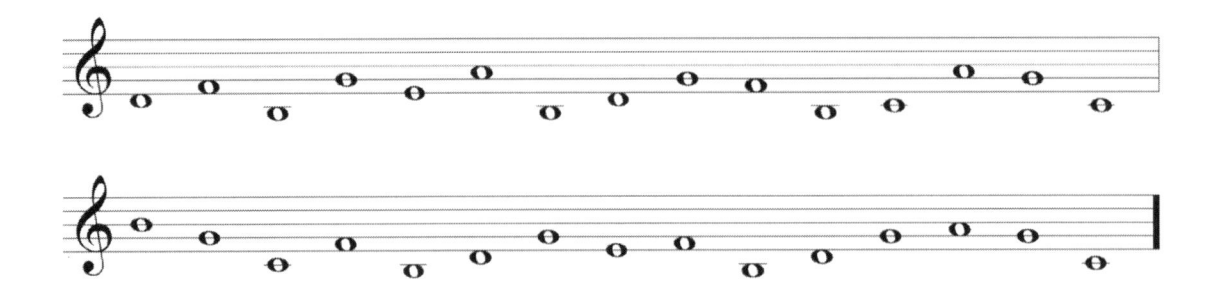

Don't forget to do this exercise in a wide variety of keys, **including minor keys**. When you do it in minor, you can (and should) play around between the natural, harmonic, and melodic minor collections.

This book focuses mainly on diatonic music, but you can feel free to include chromatic notes in these exercises. The order of chromatic notes I typically introduce is #$\hat{4}$–♭$\hat{6}$/#$\hat{5}$–♭$\hat{7}$–♭$\hat{3}$/#$\hat{2}$–♭$\hat{2}$/#$\hat{1}$ for major collections, and #$\hat{4}$–♮$\hat{3}$–♭$\hat{2}$ for minor collections (we already alternate between the natural and raised $\hat{6}$ and $\hat{7}$ when we switch between the different "mutations" of the minor collection).

This exercise is extremely effective when practiced consistently. You can even increase its effectiveness by doing it in pairs, where one person plays the notes and the other person sings back (thus forcing that person to listen with intent and figure out which note is being played). Give yourself time at first to process each note before you sing it back, but try to challenge yourself to decrease the gap of time between the played and the sung notes, and strive for a quicker reaction time.

3. Introduction to the Scale-Degrees

Summary of the Scale-Degree Exercise

- Choose a key.
- Play the tonic repeatedly in different registers, while singing back the same note in the same comfortable register (using the note name, not a solfège-syllable).
- Gradually add more scale-degrees, still playing them in different, random registers, but singing in your own comfortable register, until you have introduced the entire diatonic collection.
- **Optional** – repeat while adding chromatic scale-degrees.

This exercise should provide you with some competence in reading tonal music. As a teacher, during the process of working with this book, I expect my students to be able to sight read the melodies from the book that are tailored specifically to the scale-degrees that we are studying. However, I don't keep "real" music out of my classroom. While I don't expect them to sight-read this music, being able to do this exercise certainly gives them the ability to learn a piece of diatonic music, and I often ask them to study an excerpt and prepare it for singing in class (or in a quiz). I believe that is a reasonable expectation, which allows us the benefit of not having to exclude any music while we are in the process of mastering this skill.

4. The Dominant ($\hat{5}$) in Major Keys

Now that we are comfortable with singing melodies in stepwise motion, we shall move on to singing melodies that incorporate skips – intervals larger than a second between two adjacent notes.

In this chapter we will work on melodies that feature skips to the **dominant** scale degree ($\hat{5}$). Our initial examples will all be in the key of C major. We will move to other major keys later on.

> **Recap**: The dominant is the second most important scale-degree (after the tonic) in the diatonic collection. The $\hat{5}$-$\hat{1}$ motion in the bass is often the mark of an authentic cadence (an important tool for marking significant arrival points and establishing the tonality), which is comprised of the dominant (or dominant seventh) chord, followed by the tonic triad.

First, let us sing and memorize the following simple melodic fragment (you may use a piano for this fragment):

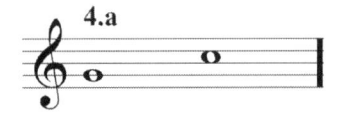

4.a

Repeat it 2-3 times until you have completely memorized it, then sing and memorize this next fragment:

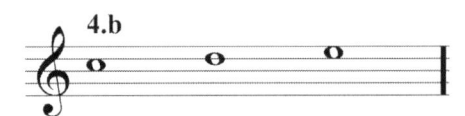

4.b

Next, we will join these two fragments into one combined fragment:

4.c

Notice that once you have memorized the first fragment, your ear remembers where $\hat{5}$ (G) is, and the relatively large interval of a major sixth between the E and the G does not

4. The Dominant (5̂) in Major Keys

make this leap difficult. To demonstrate that, we will extend this fragment by adding the note F immediately after the E:

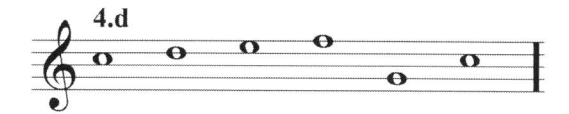

You can see that even though we sang a leap of a minor seventh, that leap did not make the fragment any more difficult to sing, since we already knew where the G was and it was not necessary to "calculate" the interval.

Let's try singing a few very short (1 measure long) melodies, which contain the G-C fragment in different surroundings:

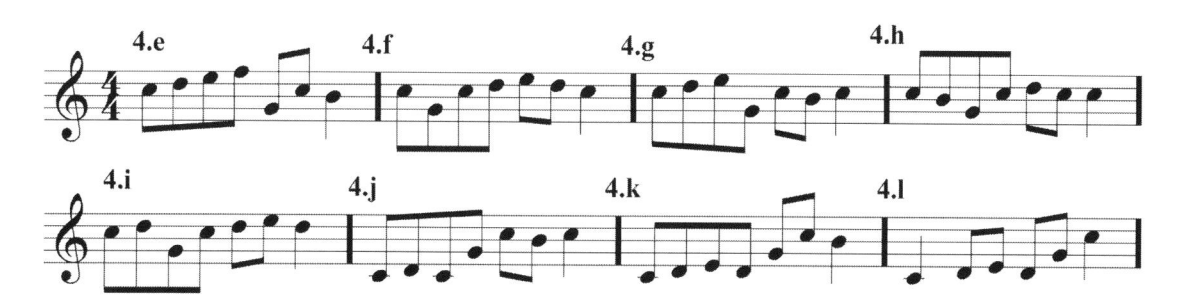

Now, let's try some longer melodies:

At this point, if you still don't feel completely comfortable with leaping to the G-C melodic fragment from any place, you should repeat the examples, and also feel free to compose and sing your own short melodies that will contain this fragment.

4. The Dominant ($\hat{5}$) in Major Keys

Once you are comfortable, you may move on to the next stage – abandoning the second note of the fragment (C) and just leaping to G, which may be followed by notes other than C. At this point, since we've only covered stepwise motion before this chapter, the only other options would be F and A.

Let's try some more one-measure examples, this time with leaps to G followed by notes other than C:

Longer Melodies in Different Keys

Now that we have experienced singing leaps to the fifth scale degree in short melodies in C major, we can try to move on to other keys. Let's look at the following example:

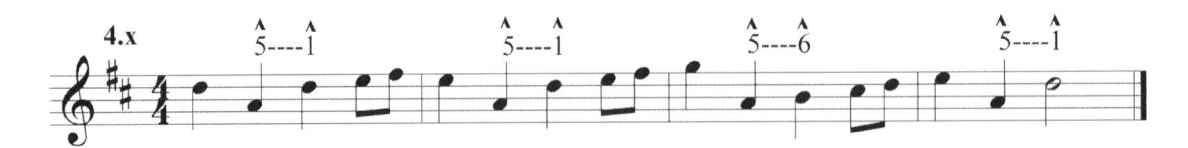

In example 4.x, we are in the key of D major. In this key, A is $\hat{5}$ and D is $\hat{1}$. This means that we treat A and D in D major **the same way we treated G and C in C major**. In measures 1, 2, and 4, we have the familiar $\hat{5}$ - $\hat{1}$ fragment, while in measure 3 we leap to $\hat{5}$ but move away from it stepwise to $\hat{6}$.

The following melodies all contain stepwise motion as well as skips to the fifth scale degree (sometimes using the 5-1 fragment). Remember, it is important to "map out" the key of each melody, and be aware of which note represents which scale-degree in that key. Your first melody is in the key of G major. Which note is $\hat{5}$ in that key? Ask yourself this question before you start each melody. Here we go:

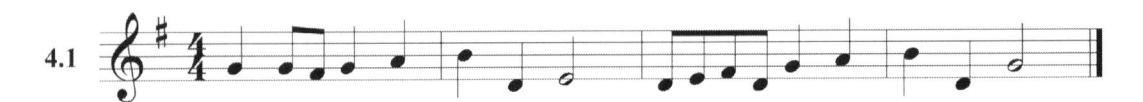

4. The Dominant (5̂) in Major Keys

4. The Dominant (5̂) in Major Keys

5. The Dominant ($\hat{5}$) in Minor Keys

Hopefully, at this point, you are feeling fairly comfortable with leaping to the dominant scale degree in major keys. Now, let's try doing the same with melodies in minor keys. We'll start by singing the same fragments we sang at the beginning of this chapter, only this time in C minor instead of C major.

Fragment #1:

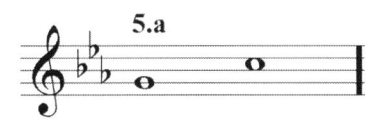

Fragment #2:

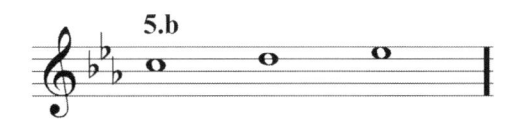

Combined fragment:

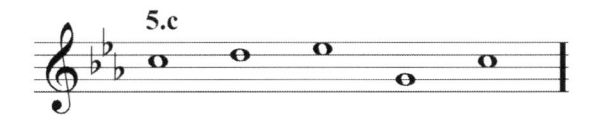

Now, we will take all of those one-measure mini-melodies we sang earlier in C-major and convert them to C-minor.

5. The Dominant (5̂) in Minor Keys

If you feel at ease with these short melodies, now is the time to move on to longer melodies in minor keys that feature skips to the dominant scale-degree. Once again, in these melodies we will start exploring keys other than C minor:

5. The Dominant (5̂) in Minor Keys

5. The Dominant ($\hat{5}$) in Minor Keys

Musical Memory Exercise: Pick a melody and sing it once or twice from the page, then turn the page over and try to sing it (or as much as you can of it) again from memory. This will not only help you acquire the skill of skipping to the fifth scale-degree and enhance your musical memory, but also train your mind to think of the "bigger picture" in the music, rather than thinking in a note-by note approach.

6. Compound Melody
Remembering the Note You Leapt From

In the last two chapters, we discussed leaps to the dominant scale-degree in major and minor keys. We will continue to work on skips to individual scale-degrees throughout this book, but before we go on, I would like to add to your repertoire of skills one very important skill: being able to identify compound melodies and keeping in mind all parts of the melody simultaneously.

A compound melody is one that embodies two or more hidden melodies in one part. The following is a very clear example of a compound melody:

6.a - From J.S. Bach's *Cantata no. 140* – *4. Chorale*

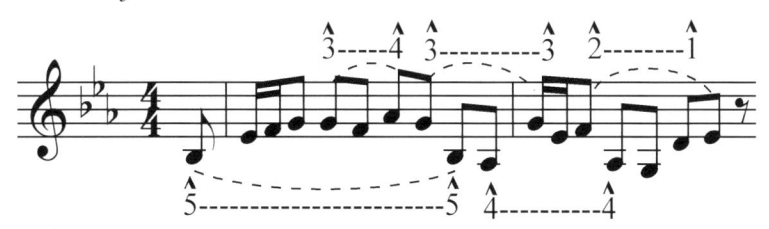

The original slurring, of course, is different. The slurs in this example demonstrate the "layers" of this compound melody. If you can retain the initial B♭ in your memory, then you can easily leap back to it on the fourth beat of the first measure. If you can retain the G in the second part of the third beat in the first measure, you will be able to go back to it at the beginning of the second measure. Of course, some notes will be more difficult to retain than others, but nevertheless, developing the skill of identifying compound melodies and retaining the sound of important notes in your memory will make your life as a musician much easier.

Here are some more compound melodies to practice. Scan each melody with your eyes before you attempt to sing it and try to identify the notes that you will attempt to retain in your memory while singing, and then start singing the melody at a **very slow** tempo, to give yourself time to think and react to the different leaps.

25

6. Compound Melody

6. Compound Melody

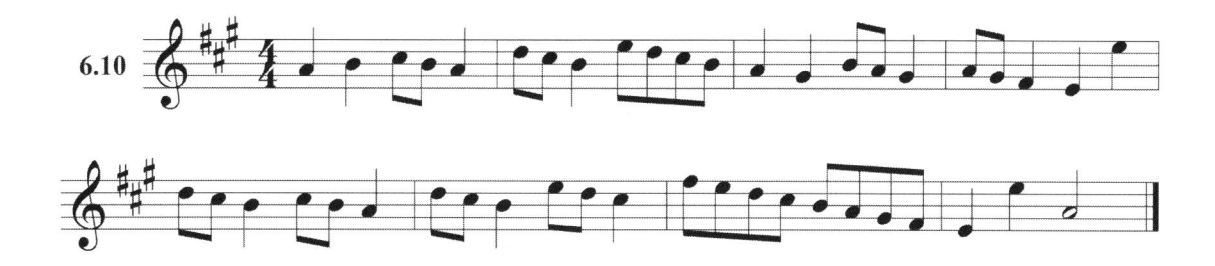

You may have found these melodies more difficult than the ones in the previous chapter. That's OK. Being able to identify a compound melody is a very important skill to have, but being able to retain notes in your ears while singing other notes is at times very challenging, and that ability is developed over time. Your main tools for working on sight-singing should be identifying each scale-degree that you leap to without relying on other notes in the music (each scale-degree will be discussed individually in the different chapters of this book). The technique discussed in this chapter is another tool that can help you, but cannot be solely relied on for sight-singing. Think of it as the "side dish", as opposed to working on individual scale-degrees, which is the "main course".

7. The Supertonic ($\hat{2}$) in Major Keys

Recap: The supertonic is the upper-neighbor to the tonic, which is the reason for its name. The supertonic may have several different roles in local contexts, but is generally considered a relatively unstable tone and is ultimately expected to resolve to the tonic.

Just like in chapters 4, we will start with examples in C major and later move on to other keys. Let's start by singing this first melodic fragment:

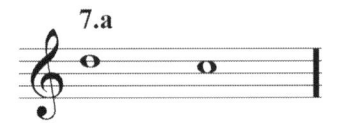

7.a

Now, let's go on to the next fragment:

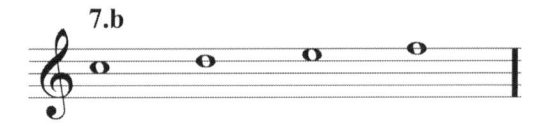

7.b

As we did in the previous chapters, we will now combine these two fragments into one longer fragment that contains a skip to the second scale-degree:

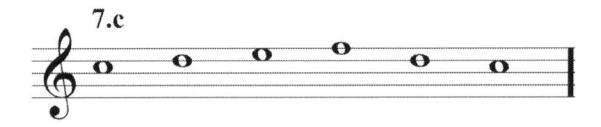

7.c

If you do not yet feel comfortable with this skip, try repeating the sequence another one or two times. If you feel confident enough, continue to the next step – short one-measure fragments:

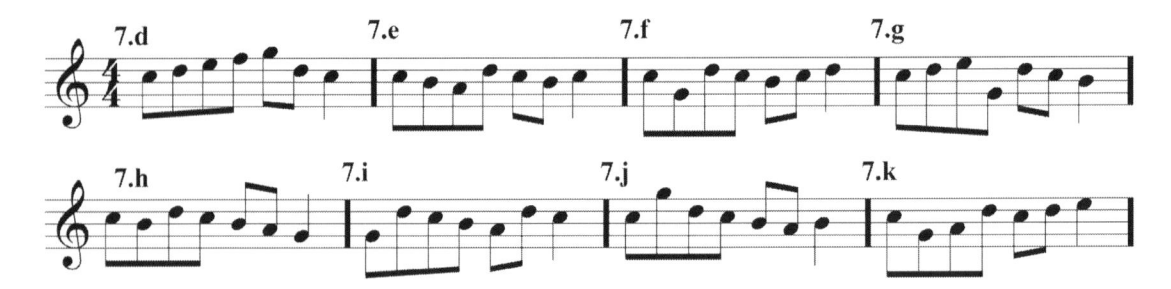

7.d 7.e 7.f 7.g

7.h 7.i 7.j 7.k

7. The Supertonic ($\hat{2}$) in Major Keys

Now for some more one-measure fragments, only this time the second scale-degree will not necessarily resolve to $\hat{1}$ (C in the case of these examples), but will possibly be followed by either stepwise motion to $\hat{3}$, or a leap to $\hat{5}$.

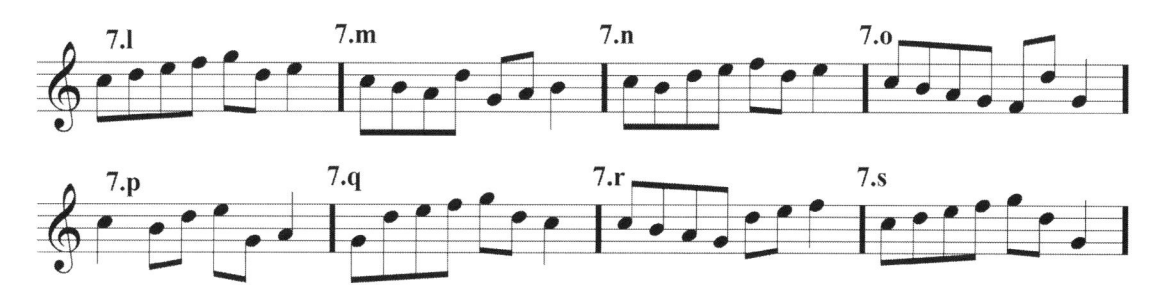

Feeling ready for some longer melodies in different keys? These following melodies will contain elements we have covered, including stepwise motion, skips/leaps to the supertonic **and** dominant scale-degrees, and compound melody elements. Once again, don't forget to "map out" your key and be aware of which note is $\hat{2}$, which note is $\hat{5}$, etc. The first melody is in D major. $\hat{2}$ in D major is the note E, and $\hat{5}$ is A. Locate these notes in the melody before you start singing, and be aware of them.

7. The Supertonic ($\hat{2}$) in Major Keys

7. The Supertonic ($\hat{2}$) in Major Keys

7. The Supertonic (2̂) in Major Keys

7.14

8. The Supertonic ($\hat{2}$) in Minor Keys

By now I'm guessing you already know the drill, so without further ado:

Initial fragments:

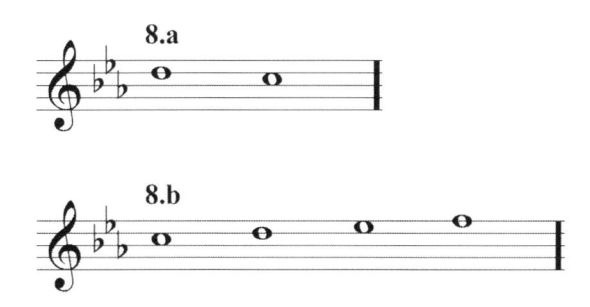

8.a

8.b

Combined fragments:

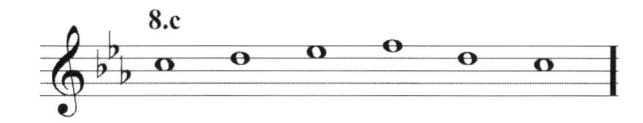

8.c

One-measure drills with leaps to $\hat{2}$ that are resolved to $\hat{1}$:

8.d 8.e 8.f 8.g

8.h 8.i 8.j 8.k

And some one-measure drills with leaps to $\hat{2}$ that will not necessarily be resolved to $\hat{1}$:

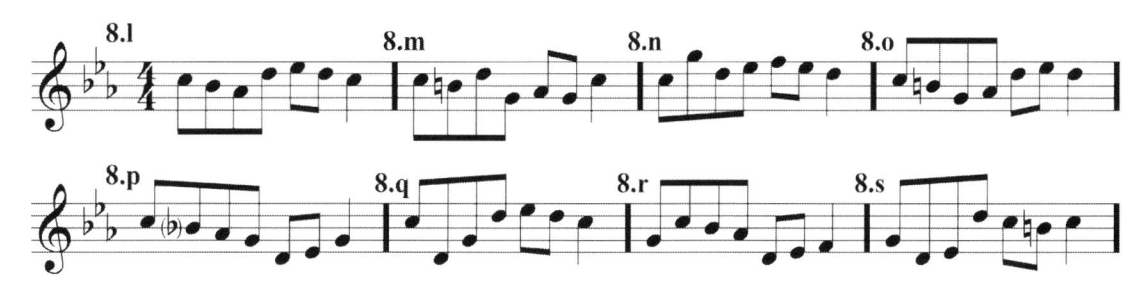

8.l 8.m 8.n 8.o

8.p 8.q 8.r 8.s

8. The Supertonic ($\hat{2}$) in Minor Keys

And finally, longer melodies in different minor keys, containing skips and leaps to $\hat{2}$ and $\hat{5}$, as well as a few compound melody spots:

8. The Supertonic (2̂) in Minor Keys

8. The Supertonic (2̂) in Minor Keys

8. The Supertonic (2̂) in Minor Keys

9. The Leading Tone ($\hat{7}$) in Major Keys

> **Recap**: The leading tone is located a half-step below the tonic, and therefore "leads" to a resolution. The leading-tone is such an important motion tool in the tonal system, that even in a minor tonality the seventh scale-degree is often altered (raised by a half-step) in order to create a leading-tone. Its role within the dominant triad is crucial for effective cadences.

Initial fragments:

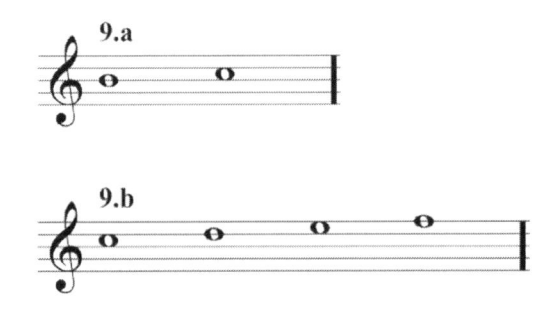

9.a

9.b

Combined fragments:

9.c

Mini-melodies, with skips to the leading tone:

9.d 9.e 9.f 9.g

9.h 9.i 9.j 9.k

9.l 9.m 9.n 9.o

9.p 9.q 9.r 9.s

9. The Leading Tone ($\hat{7}$) in Major Keys

Longer melodies in various keys, with skips to $\hat{5}$, $\hat{2}$, and $\hat{7}$:

9. The Leading Tone ($\hat{7}$) in Major Keys

9. The Leading Tone ($\hat{7}$) in Major Keys

9. The Leading Tone ($\hat{7}$) in Major Keys

9. The Leading Tone ($\hat{7}$) in Major Keys

9. The Leading Tone ($\hat{7}$) in Major Keys

9.24

10. The Leading Tone ($\hat{7}$) in Minor Keys

The minor collection in its "natural" form does not contain a leading tone. Its seventh scale-degree is positioned a whole-step below the tonic and is referred to by many music theorists as the *subtonic*. However, the subtonic is very frequently raised by a half-step and transforms into the leading tone.

There are two main advantages created by this transformation. The first, quite obviously, is that just like in major keys, the leading tone can now provide the tendency and "desire" for a tonic resolution. The other benefit is that this altered scale-degree brings with it a whole new set of intervallic relationships between itself and the other scale-degrees, including intervals such as an augmented second, a diminished seventh, a diminished fourth, and an augmented fifth. These are all intervals that do not occur in major, thus the minor now gains a more distinct character, and the "danger" of the music being perceived as in major is now practically eliminated.

We will become more familiar with the subtonic in the next chapter. However, I have decided to introduce the leading tone in minor first, mainly because it feels "natural" (no pun intended…) to follow the leading tone in major with the leading tone in minor, but also because I think it would be safe for me to say that due to the reasons I have laid out above, it is the more dominant of the two forms of the seventh scale-degree in minor.

Terminology clarification: For the purposes of this book, when discussing a generic minor tonality, the leading tone will be labeled as "$\hat{7}$" and the subtonic will be labeled as "$\flat\hat{7}$". When referring to specific minor keys, though, the scale-degree labeling will conform to the actual notes in the key. For example, the leading tone in D-minor will be labeled as "$\sharp\hat{7}$", since it represents the note C-sharp. However, the leading tone in C-minor will be referred to as "$\natural\hat{7}$", as it represents the note B-natural. Likewise, the subtonic in C-minor will be "$\flat\hat{7}$", while in D minor it will be "$\natural\hat{7}$".

10. The Leading Tone ($\hat{7}$) in Minor Keys

Initial Fragments:

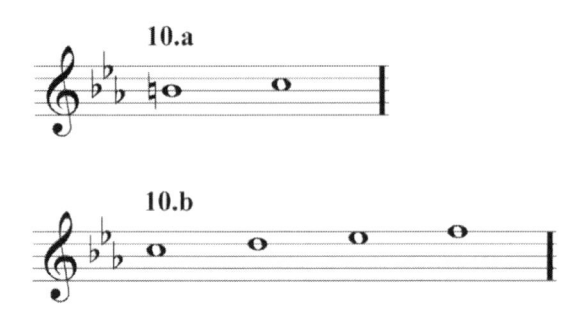

10.a

10.b

Combined fragments:

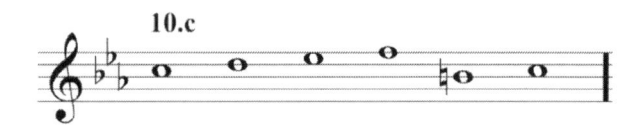

10.c

Mini melodies:

10.d 10.e 10.f 10.g

10.h 10.i 10.j 10.k

10.l 10.m 10.n 10.o

10.p 10.q 10.r 10.s

10. The Leading Tone ($\hat{7}$) in Minor Keys

Longer melodies in different keys with skips to $\hat{5}$, $\hat{2}$, and $\hat{7}$:

10. The Leading Tone ($\hat{7}$) in Minor Keys

10. The Leading Tone ($\hat{7}$) in Minor Keys

10. The Leading Tone ($\hat{7}$) in Minor Keys

11. The Subtonic (♭$\hat{7}$) in Minor Keys

In the previous chapter, we mentioned the subtonic and the various reasons for its frequent alteration and replacement by the leading tone. Nevertheless, the subtonic remains an integral part of the diatonic collection in minor, and may appear under many different circumstances in music that you will encounter. For example:

- It is common for the subtonic to appear as part of a downwards stepwise melodic motion.
- It can also be skipped to, but this would likely be in a compound melody type of situation, where it's part of a hidden stepwise melodic line.
- It is often used when a composer wishes to tonicize the relative major or modulate to it.
- It is actually very common in modal music from the medieval and renaissance periods, as well as in 19th/20th/21st Century modal music, where there is less of an emphasis on the leading tone, and a "blurry" tonality is more acceptable.
- It is very common in contemporary popular music, blues, and jazz, where there is a vast use of pentatonic collections, and it often occurs that the relative major and minor "coexist" simultaneously.

These are just a few examples, and I am sure that you will find the subtonic in other contexts as well, but the point is that we have to consider the unique character of this scale-degree in order to gain a better understanding of how it works in the diatonic minor collection and how it affects our perception of the tonality. With this in mind, let's begin our preparatory exercises:

Initial fragments:

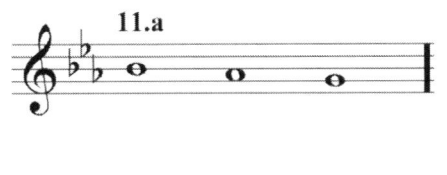

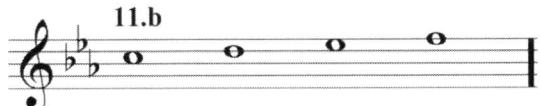

11. The Subtonic (♭$\hat{7}$) in Minor Keys

Combined fragments:

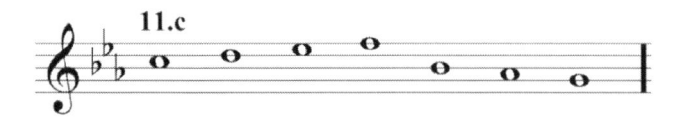

Mini-melodies:

Longer melodies in different keys, with leaps to $\hat{5}$, $\hat{2}$, $\hat{7}$, and ♭$\hat{7}$ (along with some other scale-degrees in compound melody contexts):

11. The Subtonic (♭$\hat{7}$) in Minor Keys

11. The Subtonic (♭$\hat{7}$) in Minor Keys

11. The Subtonic (♭$\hat{7}$) in Minor Keys

12. The Tonic ($\hat{1}$) in Major Keys

> **Recap**: The tonic is the first scale-degree, and the most important one of all. It is the point of reference, according to which the roles of all the other scale-degrees are defined. The tonic is considered to be the most stable note in the diatonic collection, and any tension that is built up in a piece of tonal music is expected to ultimately find its resolution in it (although in some types of music it does not).

In chapter 2, I briefly mentioned the importance of feeling the tonal center and being able to sing the tonic at any point, but I have purposely waited until this point to start working more seriously on skips to the tonic within a melody. The reason for that is, as I mentioned in chapter 3, that the tonic does not always feel as stable as a tonal center is expected to feel, and there are circumstances that make it temporarily unstable. At this point in the book, I think you will be able to identify (intuitively if not intellectually) and handle these situations.

Initial fragments:

12.a

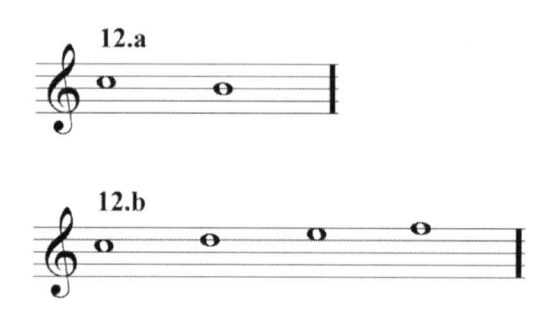

12.b

Combined fragments:

12.c

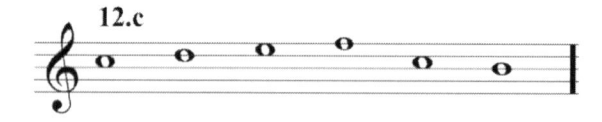

12. The Tonic (1̂) in Major Keys

Mini-melodies:

Longer melodies in different keys, with skips to 5̂, 2̂, 7̂, and 1̂:

12. The Tonic (1̂) in Major Keys

12. The Tonic (1̂) in Major Keys

12. The Tonic (1̂) in Major Keys

12. The Tonic (1̂) in Major Keys

13. The Tonic (1̂) in Minor Keys

Initial fragments:

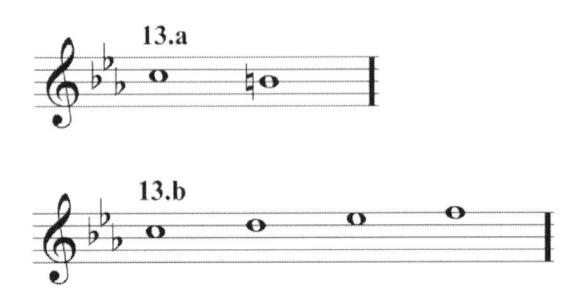

Combined fragments:

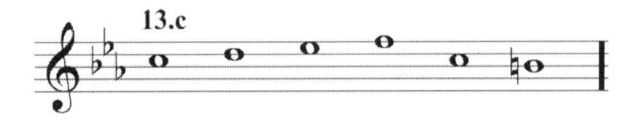

Mini-melodies:

13. The Tonic (1̂) in Minor Keys

Longer melodies in different keys with skips to 5̂, 2̂, 7̂, and 1̂:

13. The Tonic (1̂) in Minor Keys

13. The Tonic (1̂) in Minor Keys

13. The Tonic (1̂) in Minor Keys

14. The Subdominant ($\hat{4}$) in Major Keys

> **Recap**: The fourth scale-degree is called the subdominant, due to its placement, a perfect fifth below the tonic (as opposed to the dominant, which is placed a perfect fifth above the tonic). The subdominant triad often serves as a "springboard" of sorts to the dominant triad on the way to a cadence (authentic or half-cadence). However, the placement of the subdominant scale-degree a seventh above the dominant scale-degree, a tritone from the leading tone, and a half step above the mediant (in major), causes it to frequently be used as the seventh of the dominant chord, escalating tension and instability, and creating stronger expectations for a resolution to the tonic triad.

As mentioned above, the subdominant often acts as a "springboard" to the dominant. However, due to its placement, a half step above the third in major, it also has a strong tendency to pull towards the mediant (to some extent, it has a similar tendency in minor, despite being a full step above the mediant, perhaps due to association). Therefore, in this chapter we will start with two sets of isolated fragments, before we move on to the mini-melodies and longer ones.

Fragment set I

Initial fragments:

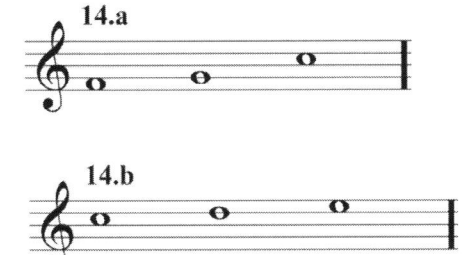

14.a

14.b

Combined fragments:

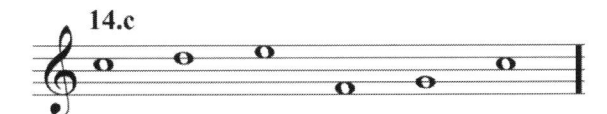

14.c

14. The Subdominant ($\hat{4}$) in Major Keys

Fragment set II

Initial fragments:

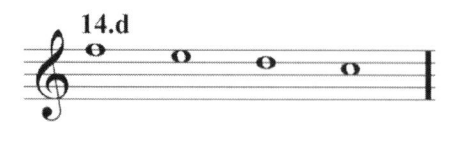

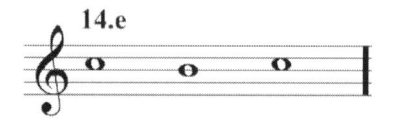

Combined fragments:

Mini-melodies:

14. The Subdominant ($\hat{4}$) in Major Keys

Longer melodies in different keys, with skips to $\hat{5}$, $\hat{2}$, $\hat{7}$, $\hat{1}$, and $\hat{4}$:

14.1

14.2

14.3

14.4

14.5

14. The Subdominant (4̂) in Major Keys

14. The Subdominant ($\hat{4}$) in Major Keys

14. The Subdominant ($\hat{4}$) in Major Keys

14.15

15. The Subdominant (4̂) in Minor Keys

As mentioned in the previous chapter, although the subdominant in minor is a full step above the mediant, it possesses a tendency towards the mediant in addition to the tendency towards the dominant, similarly to the subdominant in major keys. Therefore, we will start with two sets of isolated fragments in this chapter as well.

Fragment set I

Initial fragments:

15.a

15.b

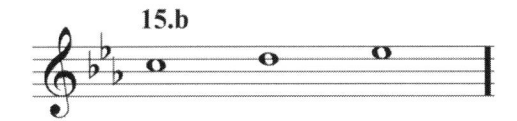

Combined fragments:

15.c

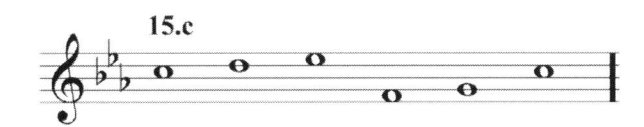

Fragment set II

Initial fragments:

15.d

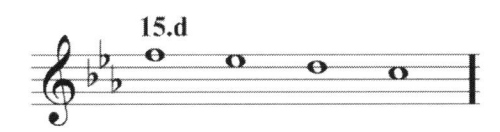

15.e

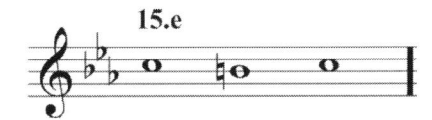

15. The Subdominant ($\hat{4}$) in Minor Keys

Combined fragments:

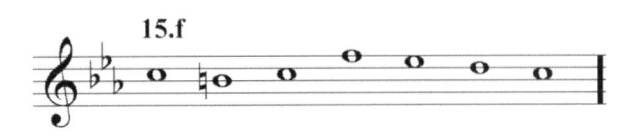

Mini-melodies:

Longer melodies in different keys, with skips to $\hat{5}$, $\hat{2}$, $\hat{7}$, $\hat{1}$, and $\hat{4}$:

15. The Subdominant ($\hat{4}$) in Minor Keys

15. The Subdominant ($\hat{4}$) in Minor Keys

15. The Subdominant (4̂) in Minor Keys

16. The Submediant ($\hat{6}$) in Major Keys

> **Recap:** Midway between the subdominant and the tonic, the submediant is an unstable tone and typically pulls towards the dominant. This is especially true in minor, where the submediant is only a half step above the dominant (as opposed to a full step in major), and serves as sort of an upper leading tone to the dominant. Similarly to the mediant, the submediant is also a factor in distinguishing between major and minor tonalities.

Initial fragments:

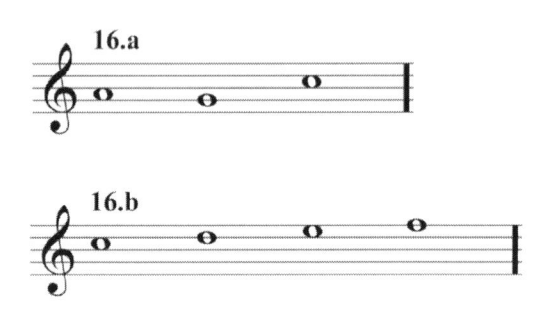

Combined fragments:

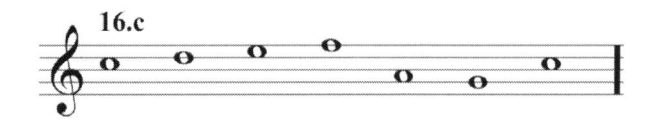

Mini-melodies:

16. The Submediant (6̂) in Major Keys

Longer melodies in different keys, with skips to 5̂, 2̂, 7̂, 1̂, 4̂, and 6̂:

16. The Submediant (6̂) in Major Keys

16. The Submediant (6̂) in Major Keys

16. The Submediant (6̂) in Major Keys

16. The Submediant (6̂) in Major Keys

17. The Submediant ($\hat{6}$) in Minor Keys

As mentioned in the previous chapter, the submediant in minor acts as an upper leading tone, of sorts, to the dominant, being only a half-step above it. It is also an important note in establishing a minor tonality, as its distance from the tonic in minor is different from the distance between the submediant and the tonic in major.

Initial fragments:

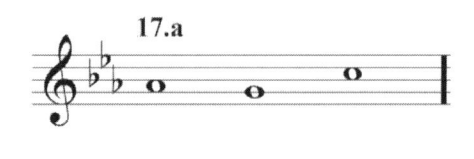

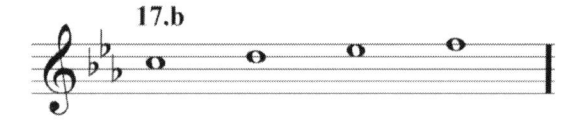

17.a

17.b

Combined fragments:

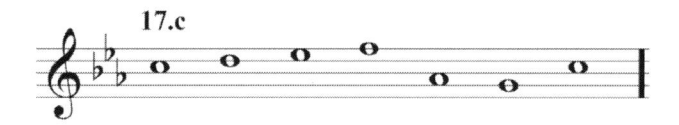

17.c

Mini-Melodies:

17.d 17.e 17.f 17.g

17.h 17.i 17.j 17.k

17. The Submediant (6̂) in Minor Keys

Longer melodies in different keys, with skips to 5̂, 2̂, 7̂, 1̂, 4̂, and 6̂:

17. The Submediant (̂6) in Minor Keys

17. The Submediant (6̂) in Minor Keys

17. The Submediant (6̂) in Minor Keys

17. The Submediant ($\hat{6}$) in Minor Keys

18. The Mediant ($\hat{3}$) in Major Keys

> **Recap**: The mediant, placed midway between the tonic and dominant scale-degrees, is considered a relatively stable tone. As the middle note of the tonic triad, it usually serves to define whether the tonic (and therefore the local tonality, in most cases) is major or minor.

As with the subdominant, we will use two sets of isolated fragments before we move on. The reason for this is that while the mediant usually tends to resolve down by step towards the tonic (through the supertonic), it also often acts as a "preliminary springboard" to the subdominant on the way up to the dominant. Both contexts are very common, thus it is helpful to keep both in mind as possibilities.

Fragment set I

Initial fragments:

18.a

18.b

Combined fragments:

18.c

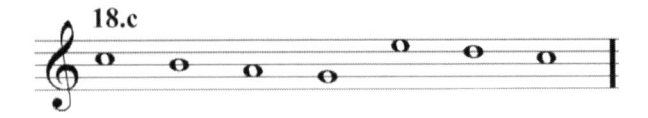

18. The Mediant (3̂) in Major Keys

Fragment set II

Initial fragments:

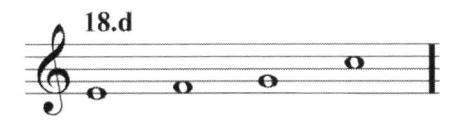

Combined fragments:

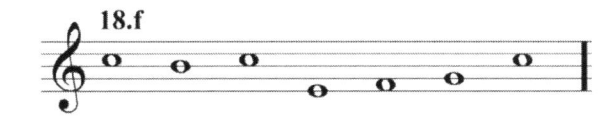

Mini-melodies:

18. The Mediant ($\hat{3}$) in Major Keys

Longer melodies in different keys, with skips to all diatonic scale-degrees, including the mediant:

18. The Mediant (3̂) in Major Keys

18. The Mediant (3̂) in Major Keys

18. The Mediant (3̂) in Major Keys

19. The Mediant (3̂) in Minor Keys

> As with the mediant in major, and for the same reasons, we will again use two sets of isolated fragments.

Fragment set I

Initial fragments:

19.a

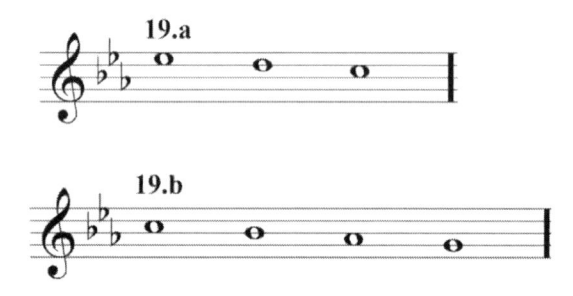

19.b

Combined fragments:

19.c

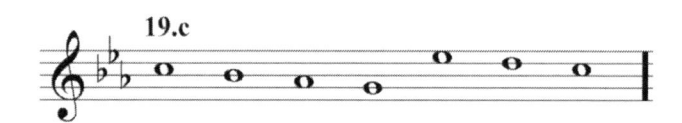

Fragment set II

Initial fragments:

19.d

19.e

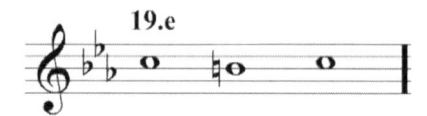

19. The Mediant (3̂) in Minor Keys

Combined fragments:

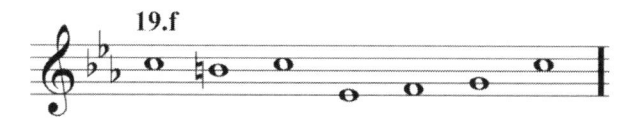

Mini-melodies:

Longer melodies in different keys, with skips to all scale-degrees, including the mediant:

19. The Mediant ($\hat{3}$) in Minor Keys

19. The Mediant (3̂) in Minor Keys

19. The Mediant (3̂) in Minor Keys

20. Stepwise Chromatic Motion

Now that we feel comfortable enough sight-singing within the diatonic collection, it is time that we took a look outside of that collection, at the notes between the diatonic scale-degrees – the chromatic notes.

The next book in this series will go deeper into this subject, and include melodies designed for practicing approaching these notes by skip, but for now, let's try to see if we can get these notes when we approach them by step. We will start with the following mini-melodies. At this point, you may use the piano as an aid if you are not sure you are singing the correct notes.

Now, let's try some more mini-melodies, this time in a minor context:

20. Stepwise Chromatic Motion

If you felt comfortable with the above mini-melodies, you should be ready for the longer melodies. Remember, these are in different keys, so the types of accidentals may differ among the different melodies. For example, the raised tonic in C major gets a ♯, while the raised tonic in B♭ major gets a ♮.

20. Stepwise Chromatic Motion

20. Stepwise Chromatic Motion

20. Stepwise Chromatic Motion

21. Tonicization and Modulations to Closely Related Keys

Although the next book in this series will go deeper into chromatic notes and their function as vehicles of tonicization and modulation, I thought it would be a good idea to touch upon this, as we are nearing the end of this book. In this chapter, we will deal with tonicization and the most common modulations – from a major tonic to the key of its dominant (i.e. from C major to G major, or from E♭ major to B♭ major), and from a minor tonic to the key of its relative major (D minor to F major, for example).

When modulating from one tonal center to another, a note from the new key will be introduced – usually one that is not part of the diatonic collection of the original key. For example, when modulating from D major to A major, the note G♯ will appear. If it's just a temporary appearance, then it might mean that the dominant has been tonicized, and the music did not modulate. However, if that note keeps appearing and the music is structured in a way that points towards the dominant as the tonal center, then a modulation is taking place, and you will most likely start to perceive all the notes as functioning in relation to the **new** tonic.

When it comes to modulating from minor to its relative major, however, there is a bit of a "problem" – the diatonic collections of both keys consist of the same notes, therefore there cannot be a "new" note. In the case of this type of modulation, the music usually reduces its utilization of the leading tone, and starts using the subtonic (♭$\hat{7}$), which in turn starts to take on a role as the dominant of $\hat{3}$ - the tonal center of the new key.

The following melodies all modulate from either a major key to its dominant, or from a minor key to its relative major. Make sure you first establish which key you are starting with, and then look for the "target key". Make a visual note of when the tonal landscape is starting to change, and pay close attention to the point at which you start to feel the music in the new key.

21. Tonicization and Modulations to Closely Related Keys

21. Tonicization and Modulations to Closely Related Keys

21. Tonicization and Modulations to Closely Related Keys

Acknowledgements

This book has been in the works for a number of years, and there are quite a few people who have been a part of this journey. First, I would like to thank Karen Fournier from the University of Michigan, who has worked with me very closely since the very beginning, encouraged me to develop my good ideas, and tactfully discouraged the bad ones. I have also been fortunate to receive expert advice and immense support from Judith Petty, Wayne Petty, and William Bolcom at the University of Michigan, for which I am eternally grateful.

I would also like to thank my colleagues Stephen Lett, Marc LeMay, Evan Ware, David Biedenbender (University of Michigan), Florie Namir (Brandeis University), and Hila Tamir-Ostrover (New York University), for testing out my materials and offering their valuable feedback.

Big thanks to my good friend and extremely talented graphic designer Lucy Namir, who designed the beautiful cover for this book.

Last, and of course not least, I would like to express my deep gratitude to my parents, Lily and Mordechai Peres, who have provided guidance and support for me in every possible way, and without whom this book would not exist.